A Peeled Wand

A Peeled Wand

Selected Poems of Anne Szumigalski

Edited by Mark Abley

With a Foreword by Elizabeth Philips

Signature Editions

Cover design by Doowah Design.

This book was printed on Ancient Forest Friendly paper.
Printed and bound in Canada by Hignell Book Printing.

We acknowledge the support of The Canada Council for the Arts and the Manitoba Arts Council for our publishing program.

Library and Archives Canada Cataloguing in Publication

Szumigalski, Anne, 1922–1999.
A Peeled Wand : selected poems / of Anne Szumigalski.

ISBN 978-1-897109-47-2

I. Title.

PS8587.Z44P44 2010 C811'.54 C2010-905617-5

Signature Editions
P.O. Box 206, RPO Corydon, Winnipeg, Manitoba, R3M 3S7
www.signature-editions.com

Contents

Part One

Part Two

Part Three

Foreword

for in that place there is neither glitter nor glare but always just enough light to read by
— *"Jerusalem"*

Anne Szumigalski's poetry is infused with spaciousness, with the far-reaching intellectual and spiritual curiosity that supports the vaulting generosity of her imagination. In *A Peeled Wand: Selected Poems*, the life of the imagination is not something fanciful, pyrotechnics that temporarily relieve us, or distract us, or otherwise reconcile us to the harsh exigencies of "real life." In Szumigalski's poetic universe, the life of the mind is the cosmic present, and we enter into this vast astonishment the moment we begin to read.

There is an extraordinary freedom in these poems, freedom to imagine other worlds, as well as worlds within worlds, and yet the work has an intimacy that is quintessentially human and ordinary, in the sense that the poems connect viscerally to the dailiness of human existence. It is this paradox, the union of the immediate and ever-changing with the everlasting, that sustains these poems, and makes them essential reading.

A Peeled Wand is both a distillation and reconfiguration of Anne Szumigalski's life's work. The poems have been arranged thematically into three sections. Roughly speaking, the first section has to do with childhood and that free access of invention that came so easily to Szumigalski. The second has to do with war and death, and the third with the spiritual, the urge to religiosity that, in this poet's work, is often shot through with humour — leavened, in some way, with wit and sly insight.

Again and again, the poet gives us access to the richness of her imagination with such ease that we understand, implicitly, that the world she has discovered is not just her world but ours as well. In the poem "The Fall," we encounter a country where the adults are trees, the children wildflowers: "A child may wake as a gillyflower and go to sleep as eglantine. Is it any wonder that, in that country, no one is in a hurry to grow up?" She enters this alternative world as effortlessly as stepping out the back door of her small house in Saskatoon to tend her garden.

This poet is able to tackle universal mysteries, such as the nature of time itself, through this union of the ordinary and the mystical. In "Fishhawks," a poem that takes place at the seaside, parents watch as time sweeps their children away from them:

> you look at me, say
> *this has all happened far too quickly*
> we wade out   I say
> *there is just time for us to bless them*
> but in that glance they have crossed the horizon
> are washed away out of our sight

After the children disappear, the parents wade back to shore:

> we two return to the beach
> the salt water drips from us
> making the dull shingles glisten
> our wet clothes cling to our legs
> behind us the sun is clouded
> the sea is cold not splendid
> *I am a widow* I tell you
> *but we are just strangers* you reply

Here time has folded over on itself. The female narrator has lost her husband, and yet at the same time, they've been returned to a point where they have not yet met and married. This very typical scenario — a family at the seaside — deftly houses that family's beginning and end.

It is this unshackling from time and space, and from the poetic conventions Szumigalski began with as a young writer — meter, conventional lineation and punctuation — that allow her work its wide range of form and content. Anne herself attributed her work's liberation to her move to the Prairies in the 1950s. In the Afterword to *On Glassy Wings* she states, "It was not so much the land that influenced me, but this extraordinary sky, a sky which has no limits but those that the poetic mind cares to put on it. If I had stayed in Britain, or indeed any part of Europe, I would certainly have written poetry all my life, but it would have been much more cramped and circumscribed, more conventional and less absurd."

She casts aside punctuation when she wants, for instance, to write with an incantatory urgency, as she does in some of her best pieces:

the soldier sees this he hears all this
as he lies there asking the earth
is this my final place my own place
("Shrapnel")

And yet she picks punctuation up again in a piece like "Halinka," in which the grief, and also a terrible kind of wonder, at the birth of a stillborn child, must be strictly confined, to make it bearable to express contradictory emotions in just a few lines: "For you, there never was such a thing as a face. There were hands and fingers, curled feet with curled toes. There was a heart in your chest, red and whole as a candy, and a white iris growing in the place of your understanding." With this last phrase, the lifeless child is returned to the garden.

To Anne Szumigalski, gardening and the writing of poetry were closely allied. "It is just with these two things," she said to me more than once, "that I can start out in the morning, and look up when I'm done to find that evening has come." Writing, she entered a realm of timelessness, as she did amidst the poppies in her garden, and that elasticity in the nature of space and time appears in poems as different as "In the Wilderness" and the untitled poem that is an excerpt from her play, *Z: A Meditation on Oppression, Desire and Freedom.* In the latter, time has dissolved under conditions of extreme deprivation and cruelty:

Once I was a child and once I was a woman,
A woman in a cage, a lynx in a trap.

I was my own mother and I nursed myself.
I was my own child and I suckled myself…

This is Szumigalski at her most elegiac. Many of her poems about death, loss and even war have a note of lightness in them, either outright humour or a sense of the rich incongruities of existence. This lightness lets us hover over the edge of the abyss without falling, without succumbing to that blackness. Here, writing about the Holocaust, there is no room for any kind of relief: time has collapsed entirely, causing this most excruciating contortion of mother and child.

Szumigalski's work is deeply, abidingly humane. It covers the entire span of the human experience, from birth through to death, while always allying itself with the wisdom and grace of the imagination.

It is ten years, as of this writing, since Anne Szumigalski's death at age 77. The poems have a flexion, a lithe musicality, a depth of sensibility and revelation, and these qualities do not diminish over time, but seem to strengthen, become more insistent with each passing year.

If you care to listen for it, you will hear the clear notes of her instrument, the trembling sound of her young voice echoing in the bare hills, sighing in the branches of every tall tree.

("Voice")

A Peeled Wand: Selected Poems is an important addition to Canadian literature because we have a voice in Anne Szumigalski that is both youthful and timeless. And because she shows us that the simple questions are often the most complex and the least answerable.

The question is which
Of these days was first
Which will be the last?

("Old Woman in Winter")

My darling seedling will you flourish?

("Malus")

Must I become my own child
And rock myself to sleep in my own arms?

(Untitled, from *Z*)

There was no road and no direction. Would there ever be again?

("Viaticum — The Text")

There is immeasurable pleasure and reward in reading and rereading these poems, in struggling, along with the poet, toward answers to the questions that taunt and electrify us, answers that loom and yet recede. In Anne Szumigalski's poetry, we are given rich and varied and tenacious inquiries; she gives us dreams, desires, puzzles, insights, sorrows, revelations, epiphanies. The answers recede and, as she says in "Untitled ('when earth leaps up')," "all we have left is the question." Her work teaches us to accept mystery, to journey on without explication or conclusion, going farther and farther into and out of ourselves. These poems will engage the imaginations of faithful and new readers for many years to come.

— *Elizabeth Philips*

Part One

Our Sullen Art

the language of poetry has something to do
with the open mouth the tongue that jumps
up and down like a child on a shed roof calling
ha ha and who's the dirty rascal now?
the same boy sent to his room for punishment
leans from his window listening for animals
far away in the woods strains his ears to catch
even the slightest sound of rage but nothing howls
even the hoot of owls in the dusk is gentle

he hears the tiny snarl of the shrew
the rasp of the snail's foot on the leaf
the too-high squeaking of bats which comes
to his head as the vibration
of distant hacksaws   he hum humms
with his lips tight shut he stands there
listening and humming almost through the short night
then   falls into the tangle of sheets and blankets
where fitfully he sleeps while slowly
the window greys to four panes of bleak light

the day's first traffic travels carefully
past the windows and doors of the shut house
so as not to awaken in the child
those savage cries our violent
our pathetic language of poems

Annwfn

for T.H.

a world in the shape of an egg
lies in the palm of the hand

which warms it and the warmth
brings out the sheen of the eggshell

you stare at its wholeness which you know
is present only from moment to moment

in your other hand in a nest of worn fingers
lies another egg which you see as exactly like

the first but the fingers know the difference
for this one is withdrawn from its chalky shell

into its chill yolk   cannot
be warmed at a touch

god hold me to myself you cry out departing
not comprehending how you will pass through

that wall thin as eggshell to where
everything seems exactly as it was at home

yet there is a difference
if only you could put your hand on it

in the morning the farmwife comes from the house
her apron full of wheat

or what passes for wheat until the sun
hits it and it sparkles   handfuls

of crystals thrown up never to fall
while the silly hens gobble at nothing

and the young woman erased for a moment
by the dazzle of the sun

turns and becomes that other girl
rosy and solid whom you left years ago

The Fall

My father was born in a distant country where every person is a tree — every adult that is.

Children are fieldflowers, they are grass, they are lilies and poppies and small blue lupines. Until puberty, they are any plants they choose. More than that, they may change their minds as many times as they wish. A child may wake as a gillyflower and go to sleep as eglantine. Is it any wonder that, in that country, no one is in a hurry to grow up?

At the age of twelve or so, each must name a tree and is stuck with this choice until the tree falls from age, or is struck down by the axe of the woodcutter. This last is their way of explaining the death of the young in battle, for, in spite of their worship of the peaceable plant, they are a warlike lot.

All this my father told me, but though I bothered and cajoled him, he would never say which tree he had chosen or whether, in this new country, he still felt bound by the customs of his birthplace.

He always seemed just a man to me, and very like other people's fathers: that is, strong and infallible in my childhood and, as I advanced into adolescence, more and more clumsy and overbearing.

There was one difference though. Unlike other men he was never seen without a shirt or a sweater. Not that he was particularly modest in other ways. Several times I caught him pulling on his trousers in a hurry. I had a good look. Nothing strange there. But what was he hiding beneath his T-shirts and button-up cardigans? Was he afraid of woodpeckers? Was there a hole there, beneath his heart, where a squirrel had made her nest?

I was almost a grown woman when he took me for a holiday in a warmer part of the country. It was May and already early summer in that gentle climate. He pointed out a tree I had never seen on the Prairies and acknowledged it as his own. *Hippocastanum* he explained proudly. Its leaves were huge green hands, and between them sprung tall racemes of bloom like white and yellow candles. This then was my father's tree, generous in its spread, amazing in its summer complacency.

We stood there, hand in hand, as he told me about its various phases, of how in fall it would bear inedible brown nuts in leathery green cases, nuts that are the weapons of little boys in their battles.

All this was years ago, and my father is dead now, hollowed and fallen like every tree before him. I was with him when he died.

No sooner had he taken his last breath than I leaned over him and began to unbutton his pyjama jacket. What did I expect to find? Simply the chest of an old tired man, the tangles of coarse grey hair intricate as twigs, the nipples hard and resinous as winter buds.

Third Trimester

The gibbous moon in the trees is the head of
a child slipping out between sturdy thighs,
lying under bent and bloodied knees. Every
twig is a coarse hair, pubic, female, innocent.

But the moon is nothing but folded paper, the
Old Man explains, wielding his scissors over
the crisp white sheet, *or a handful of coins,*
the quarters one by one pushed into the slitted
back of a pot pig, or maybe a sacred wafer
shoved between the clenched teeth of a nun.

Then I told him of when I was brought to bed.
Clouds close-wrapped the body of my child.
They were a net of fine-knotted threads.
Small fingers, small toes kept getting caught
in that web.

The moon wavered in the mist, the wind
moithered like a wailing babe, when the head,
wet as though rained-on, squeezed out through
a slit no bigger than a shrieking mouth.

And the cut rope, and the dark blood
trickling, and the little daughter at last
lying in the lap of the sun.

Halinka

It is right, they say, to bury a stillborn child with a mirror on the pillow beside her. That way, at the resurrection, when she opens her eyes for the first time, she will see her face and recognize herself.

But that's not for you, little daughter, little flaccid creature. For you, there never was such a thing as a face. There were hands and fingers, curled feet with curled toes. There was a heart in your chest, red and whole as a candy, and a white iris growing in the place of your understanding.

Your Child Looks Up

Your child looks up at you, offers her hand
the empty one

She holds it flat, straight-fingered
every crease outlined in dirt

Dust of the Earth made sticky
with the sweat of effort
a whole afternoon at play

Are you daring enough
to take such a hand

After all where has it been

Stroking caterpillars, probing drains
stirring pond ooze, scratching
her hot little bum

Ah but hasn't she caught you
in your own web of speculation

Just so you won't ask what's
in the other fist hidden
in her drooping knit sleeve

A stallion, an island, an iceberg
a straw hat with green feathers
a train where all the passengers are pigeons

A forbidden book with fine white paper
between glossy colour plates

Don't be so poetic, keep to the prophetic
It's her desire she is hiding

Her desire for the death of her brother
conceived in your bed last night

Fear of Knives

The young woman stands by the window holding something up to the light. It could be a feather from the wing of a dove. It could be the leaf of that lily plant whose blossom heavy with scent bends almost to the earth, something she could certainly see through the clear pane if she stood on a chair and looked out.

If the light should fall on this thing, she believes, it will either melt into itself or into the idea of itself, a dagger, that is, a kris, a bright blade.

Soon twilight will fill every part of the room. It will creep out from the corners hiding the pattern on the wallpaper, which is parrots in a tropical forest, hiding the dusty squares where pictures once hung in their frames, in their glory.

She imagines the paintings as battle scenes with horses and chariots and flashing swords, or perhaps the smaller ones were simply illustrations torn from the *Book of Weapons*, badly framed and hung slightly askew. Why, she asks, did no one bother to straighten them?

Once, in another house, when they were children, her brother was given a skinning knife for Christmas. She remembers how envy filled up her mind like sour cranberry juice in a cup. She had plotted to somehow wrest that knife from him, but all day he kept it buttoned in the pocket of his jerkin, safe in its sheath.

At night it lay under his pillow with his other treasures, a white stone with a hole in it big enough for a little finger to poke through, a worn Clovis point he had found one day on the pathway to school. These things were of no interest to his sister whose one desire was the blade with the elk-horn handle.

Dark falls at last, and the woman remembers both her desire and her fear. How, if she managed to thrust her hand under the pillow and steal away the knife, she had planned to bury it in a hole in the garden. How she had planned to tell herself as she covered the sharp curve of the blade with damp earth that she was hiding her brother in a place where no one would ever find him again.

Childermas

1

a word meaning Holy Children
has been lost
between the pages of a book

one early dusk
you lean over my shoulder
the better to see what I am reading
you riffle through the pages with your thumbs
and that forgotten sound escapes into the world
through the fan of leaves

at once we begin trying
to pronounce it
the long and difficult vowels
rest on our lips like stinging insects
we dare not brush away

then the computer gets hold of it
flaps the syllables about
cards follow cards
sliding out
and piling up

and on the cards the punched names
of daughters and of sons
their many variations
from century to century
from language to language

2

the Madonna whose smile
is as sweet as plaster
turns out to be made
of painted wood
her stiff crinoline
is carved as well as painted
perhaps to hide the hinges
that pin her skirts together

a bent sexton with floppy hair
fits in the tiny key
so delicately made
a brass scroll

the saints, children of Mary,
live beneath her skirts
there they stand in stiff rows
palms raised together in a prayer
one row for martyrs
one for prelates
another for pinched abbesses
who have given it all up

at the very centre
where Mary's legs (if she had any)
would spring from her body
winged innocents play among vines
and ears of carved wheat

the true heart of the Madonna
remarks the sexton
with sacred joy

3

one Sunday in May our children
who have hardly noticed us till now
decide on a Feast of Recognition

the youngest brings chains of withering marigolds
twines them over the backs of our chairs
the two eldest, with napkins over their arms,
bring in the dinner course by course
the food, thank goodness, is invisible
we gesture over huge empty plates
our daughter, not spilling a drop,
pours red ink into the glasses for wine

the last course is a much more solemn affair
we are told to rise and all together sing

the muddled singing gives a mewling sound

then a dish of flames is set down before me
its cinders glowing like cherries
you are luckier
get a basket of petals
into which you dip your face
making munching noises

you come up smiling
crushed petals cling to your hair

who is to blame for my lips' blisters?

afterwards your cool mouth
tastes of almonds

A Child and His Mother Camp Out on a Cool Night

The child putting his hands together thinks his prayer is like a pancake his mother has baked for him. She poured batter on a hot stone and when the edges curled she folded it and placed it between his fingers. And the pancake is a flower folded at sunset, and the flower is a nest hidden in a tree and the nest hung there in the sky is a dark star.

If you want light, his mother tells him, you must pray for it. Shine this flashlight to your ear and it will brighten the inside of your skull. You'll see light through to the forests of the mind, where birds sleep all night in their nests in the trees and stars hang down from the branches like icicles.

Frances Walking like a Crane

one morning in a house in the country
a child rises older than her mother
she combs her hair and braids it
then she begins setting the kitchen to rights
she sweeps the floor rinses and stacks the dishes
each with its wreath of washed-away pink roses

mother is skipping about in the yard
under the trees over the annual border
just as though it didn't matter treading on the flowers
then she sits down by the fishpond
splashes her feet in the shallow water
each foot has a smudged red mark
where the shoe has pinched the joint

the cat comes padding delicately over the grass
the woman picks it up and strokes its flat black fur

from the house the girl follows
stalking in high white boots
holding before her a saucer of milk
carefully warmed

Sandblind at the Crossing

in the distance she sees a very tall dog
a great dane with a narrow elegant muzzle

in the distance he sees a print sack
blowing on the line

he sees a boat with a calico sail
the wind blows her across the intersection

the dog comes nearer and is a thin-legged boy
carrying a delicate cat with cobalt eyes

this woman the boy thinks
dressed in a meadow of flowers
is an old white-haired animal
the smell of her skin
still flavoured with breastmilk

the woman wants to greet the child
but simply inclines her head
she cannot bring herself to speak

he's disappointed for he had meant
to tell her the story of his stolen cat

how he's taught it to caress his face
with unsheathed claws

not really scratching
but leaving long strokes
of soft white down his olive cheek

On Being a Stranger

Today on this side of the lake
Two young boys icefishing

They bring me a needly pickerel,
They bring me mail from town.

Are you the foreign woman?
The small one asks me

I am, I answer, the foreign woman
Though I haven't moved from this place
For twice as long as you've lived

Yet I am truly a stranger, not quite
At home anywhere.

Always some part of me
Away in another country.

I hand them two jars of sweet berries,
Two spoons. They won't come in

Stand outside in the snow
With berry juice oozing
From the corners of their mouths

I watch them from the doorway
My hands slowly unsealing your letter.

In Praise Of My Own Breasts

And why, you ask, do I have this bosom like a shelf. You mean a shelf of land, shading the water at the base of a cliff. The sea has eaten what's underneath as the tide comes and goes swallowing chalk and flints.

It's not like that. I think this bust is a thicket of sharp thorns, yet brave birds do make their nests here. They bring soft hay and the blond hair of young nuns when it's time to cast off their novitiate, at Lammas when they make their final vows. The leaves of the breasttree shelter the chicks from rain and it's warm here close to the heart of things.

And I've had it said that my breasts are twin puddings stirred by the hand of God. That is when he gets up to his old tricks in the fall. The pudding cloth covers sweet plums and spices, come Christmas will the cloths burst as they did last year in the boiling?

A lover told me one breast is a giant puffball the other a coconut. One is full of sweet milk the other of ripe spores. He didn't say which he admired the most. Another fellow whittled them down, one to a sweet pippin the other to a sour baking apple. I didn't invite him in to do the cooking.

I'm getting old and they've softened now, a mouse family or a small swarm of bees could hide behind these things, but they're not finished yet. I've heard you can make two wallets from any dead granny's dugs. Me, when I go I'll bequeath you a couple of saddle bags, capacious and serviceable, lined with soft feathers and green leaves. Fastened with hooks and eyes.

Crabseeds

A man I used to know
Has become my child
One day his mouth grew hard and small
Trying not to let me catch him smiling

From caress of finger
From breathy sticky kiss
He got nothing but a command
To sleep and sleep over
From day to day

Pips in an apple rattle
Like the hurt seeds of his mind
Under his low tread
The fruit breaks and opens
And shells out from sharp capsule
Its small brown stones

Bring me an old plate
And set it under the tree
I want to arrange the crabseeds
So as to resemble
Some kind of disorder

It Wasn't a Major Operation

the surgeon joined us
with a long wire he threaded
through your left earhole
and into my right one

when we woke up from the anaesthetic
we had to begin practicing at once
every time you nodded your head
I inclined mine
we bobbed together this way and that

when the wire was too taut
there was a knotted feeling in my head
when it was too slack
it looped and caught in my necklace

but now we have got used to
the continual lolling motion
and are able to go
for a short walk every day

this morning while we were
admiring the lilies
a row of birds sat down on our wire

night has fallen now
and they are still here
nine sparrows and a kingbird

The Prisoner

A man looks down into the handsome blue eyes of the woman he is making love to. In her left eye he's surprised to see a tiny man very much like himself, only this one is fully dressed in cotton trousers and a blue jacket and is sitting dejectedly on a three-legged stool. His arms are folded across his chest.

The woman blinks her eyes, and it seems to the man that her dark lashes are the bars of the jail cell that the tiny fellow is locked up in. *You have a prisoner in your left eye,* says the man to his mistress. She doesn't understand but imagines that the remark must be some sort of compliment, for after all he *is* making love to her. *How happy I am with you,* she murmurs, looking vaguely and ecstatically up at him.

The man cannot take his mind off the poor little captive. But still he is in the act of making love, and so he moans softly to show his mistress how much pleasure she is giving him.

When the woman again opens her eyes, she sees her lover leaning over her, gazing intently into her face. *Come here,* he says brusquely, and taking her head roughly between his hands he jerks it towards him. Startled by his coldness and violence, the woman begins to weep with indignation.

Keep still you bitch, shouts the man. When at last he succeeds in holding down her head and turning back her left eyelid, there is nothing there but a blue eye, its edges red with fury. The man has never felt so chagrined. He scrabbles about amongst the bedclothes, searching for the tears his mistress has just shed. Perhaps the little man, who looks so much like himself, is drowning somewhere between the crumpled sheets.

Long Distance

My wife left me
When we were both quite young
She said she was going to visit her cousin
There must have been more to it than that

Last summer she came back
Just before harvest
I awoke and she was there
Baking pies in our wedding dishes

She's a gray and folded woman now
Even her lips are creased
But sometimes when she sits there phoning
A curve of her cheek or arm
Reminds me of the girl she once was

What good is that to me?
I want to remember her always
As she is now

Fishhawks

my son stands in waist-high water
the salt reddens his skin
out of his face spring wiry hairs
thickening to a beard
his arms have become wide and heavy

he splices rope
smells of the tar that blackens his fingers
he has learned to make his living from the sea

(the huge shadow of a bird
darkens the sand around us
I speak, say to you *look*
at that rare creature
an osprey)

further out from the shore
your daughter is a rock
jutting from the waves
she is rounded and hollow
within her is a sea-cave
her face is a pearly shell
a shining operculum
stoppers up her mouth
her singing is muffled, a murmur

the boy smiles
his semen darts out of him
a shoal of swift fishes
entering her secret place
he stretches out his finger
flicks away the shell plug from her mouth
so that she may cry out

you look at me, say
this has all happened far too quickly
we wade out   I say:
there is just time for us to bless them

but in that glance they have crossed the horizon
are washed away out of our sight

we two return to the beach
the salt water drips from us
making the dull shingles glisten
our wet clothes cling to our legs
behind us the sun is clouded
the sea is cold not splendid
I am a widow I tell you
but we are just strangers you reply

out there where the great bird hovers
mantling preparing to spiral
there is a faint wailing

In the Wilderness

We decided to sleep out on the prairie
zipped naked in one bag
no tent between us and the distant sky

I dreamt we aged quite a bit
our hair grew brittle
our legs got thinner

The wind began to blow

It blew up a gritty storm

We said we ought to get up
and stamp out the fire

The high wind rolled us against a fencepost

A pagewire thorn caught in the skin of my arm

And still we only dreamt the storm and the darkness
nothing could rouse us up out of the grass
until morning when a few flakes of snow
fell on my sleeping hands which were
still gripping the blankets

and the flakes fall and melt on my sleeping hands
each one as it melts staining me
with the tawny stain of speckled age

I cry out in fear
the touch of the snow is like an acid burn

and there you stand in your strength
showing your proud cluster of gray Jupiter curls
you dress slowly
you are not even cold in the cold morning
your feet redden in the white grass

I braid my hair

you gently balance a roof of wet twigs
over the ashy fire

A Game of Angels

Look at me I say
to your face on the pillow
to your eyes with their straight glossy stare

I move my arms up and down to remind you
that I am that woman who once came
with armfuls of ferns, with armfuls
of branches, bunched them and
pinned them to the shoulders
of your tunic, trying to persuade you
to flap and fly upwards
out of this cup of earth
between the mountains

Remember I say
those sundays we spent
in a tent of sheets
testing our hold on each other
caressing with silky pinions
one another's flesh
how our mouths' soft beaks
gave off cries like battling doves
or other fierce creatures

The eagle for instance
flying upwards
until the sun irked our watching eyes
as it flashed between
those specks of wings

When the bird fell
on gopher or prairie mouse
we could hear the air
whistling through its claws
and you smiled

as you do now
grasping the blankets
with old talons

Part Two

Voice

How to begin a story at the end, when the battle is fought and lost, and crows are picking the bones of all flesh?

A young woman, her head covered, her feet bare, wanders on the battlefield among the fallen, wanders here and there looking for the corpse of her brother, her lover, but how can she find him amongst all this rotting flesh, these whitening bones?

At noon a hawk spirals down and drops a cold blue eye at her feet. This she recognizes as the keen right eye of her beloved. At midnight an owl flies silently past and lets fall a tangle of sinews in a thornbush nearby. These she knows were once his heartstrings. These scattered bones about her feet are all that is left of his body.

The woman picks up the skull. Over and over she kisses that cold and empty mouth. Then she scrabbles amongst the long bones and the wide, seeking what she needs for her purpose. From kneebone and thigh, from handbone and rib, she fashions an ivory harp and strings the harp with the sinews and begins to play on it.

As for the eye, that she fits back into its bony socket, and the skull she hangs among the thorns so that it may gaze out forever on that desolate plain, the scene of the destruction of so much youth and strength. And she calls on the rain and the snow to give their tears to weep for what might have been between faithful lovers.

If you care to look for them, you may find her footprints in the dewy grass, in the desert sand, on the leafy floor of the forest.

If you care to listen for it, you will hear the clear notes of her instrument, the trembling sound of her young voice echoing in the bare hills, sighing in the branches of every tall tree.

When the mist rises you may even catch a glimpse of her standing windblown on a bare rock by the sea, for hasn't she sworn to journey the whole world over playing her wild harp, singing her sad songs? And thus she will ever wander and sing while there are soldiers fallen in battle and lovers left to grieve.

Shrapnel

shrapnel has torn the man's ribs apart
there is a shabby wound in his breast
his mouth opens innocently upon a cry

he wants to curse his enemies but cannot
for he sees them as striplings lying in the grass
each with a girl beneath him
the long grass full of clover and fieldherbs
waves gently in the heat
the men get up from the women
and buckle on their belts
the women just lie there looking up at the thundery sky
we are wounded with joy they tell each other
we are happy happy happy

the soldier sees this he hears all this
as he lies there asking the earth
is this my final place my own place
he glances upwards to where
the tops of the trees almost meet
there is just a small patch of empty sky showing
it must be spring for a bird with a straw in its beak
swoops down to a low bough   he tries to think
of the name of the bird
he tries to think of his own name
the name of his son who has learned to speak already
so his wife writes   he has seen the child only once
and that was more than a year ago

he tries to remember the colour of his wife's eyes
he sees only her frailty those little narrow birdbones
beneath the soft flesh
he wishes she was another woman
one easier to abandon   one calm and robust
with a wide smooth brow

but who could forget that pitiful teat
in the child's mouth

the curious maze of blue milkveins whose pattern
he traces in the dirt   his hand touches a broken brick
here was a house   now he remembers the collapse
of its walls

he licks his lips tasting for brickdust
he counts his strong teeth with his tongue
they are all there unchipped   he hears the bland
voice of the dentist telling him he has perfect bite

he shuts his eyes against the light but it shines on
through rosy lids which are the same colour exactly
as his wife's secret he wants to part her legs
and touch her glistening vermillion lining
now at last he understands
why he loves the bodies of women
more than the bodies of men   for pale skin covers
a man all over and only a wound can show his lining

carefully he passes his hands over his body
buttoned into its tunic of stiff drab wool
until he finds the hole in his chest
he thrusts in his fist to staunch the blood
a pulse beats close to his folded fingers
it is insistent and strong
it is pushing him away from himself

Sitting Under Death's Rich Shade

in June I visited a charnel house
in Holland I was searching
for a friend   I wore black gloves
the attendant showed me great respect

it is tidy in there
smells faintly of the dark earth
at Easter the members of the Sepulchre Society
polish up the bones and arrange
them in order of rank and sanctity

I was looking for a huge bony skull
with a small round hole
in the left temple
— a healer had once trephined the head
to let out evil —
when I had found him
I knotted him into my kerchief
and carried him home

Frans I began
I have so much to tell you
will you or won't you hear
my confession?

he was silent   smiled sadly

Frans I told him
may I say at last
that once I desired you?   a bit
of me is broken
because of your memory

no tears fall from dead eyes
his grin becomes toothy, lascivious

damn you I cry out
you would not take me
when I was fifteen and dangerous

The Name of Our City

in the town square
her hair like a flock
of pigeons flies
up from the clippers
one feathery tuft remains
someone has pinned
a paper to her smock
says something absurd about
fraternizing
who is the enemy?
I ask   she tries to open
eyes swollen to slits
from weeping

just a man she says
and I notice the freckles
on her hands   this is
the first time
I have seen her

she follows me everywhere
to the beer parlour
to the poolhall
but the man's a barber
so we soon get out of there
to Tilly's where one of the girls
tries to lend her a hat
she follows as though
we were fastened together
with a rope

a passer-by remarks
that the rope is invisible
I am surprised
it feels heavy enough
and when I look down
there it is
yellow as plaited tow

she follows me to the end of town
past ducks swimming on an oily
dugout   to the dump
and there is her hair
dark fronds and single strands
strewn about on soapflakes boxes
and over some sodden plates
and cups of copper-coloured paper

when we come to a grimy hut
naturally we go in together
but she stands so long
staring through the cloudy
pane of window
that the set of her features
becomes blurred in my mind

at last she turns
and lays her cold self down
on the broken cot
fear-streamers ray from her head

and a mouth opens
it is a small dark hole
her face is greyer
than the pillow

Untitled (poem for female voice)

from the play Z: A Meditation on Oppression, Desire and Freedom

And I'll tell you again and again the same story,
Once I was a child and once I was a woman,
A woman in a cage, a lynx in a trap.

I was my own mother and I nursed myself.
I was my own child and I suckled myself.
Sometimes in my sleep I saw a house.
Sometimes a fire warmed my dreams.

Once I ate a chocolate dream cake.
Once my lover came to me.
That's when I died and was burned.
Nothing, nothing remains of me but ashes in the wind.

They have snatched away my child.
They have broken him against the wall.
Is there no one to avenge him?

The bones of the innocent are trampled underfoot.
They are scoured by the wind.

Must I become my own infant
And hold myself against my own breast?
Must I become my own child
And rock myself to sleep in my own arms?

And I'll tell you again and again the same story,
Once I was a child and once I was a woman,
A woman in a cage.
I was my own mother and I nursed myself.
I was my own child and I suckled myself.
Sometimes in my sleep I saw a house.
Sometimes a fire warmed my dream.

Once my lover came to me,
But his bones were twigs.

His breath was gravel in my mouth.
That's when I died and was burned.
Nothing remains of me
But a handful of ashes in the wind.

Looking for Uncle Tich in the War Cemetery

o tenderness of heaven rain down on army tombstones this is the song the band plays while under the sun spiders are crawling up hot marble a time to crawl up   a time to swing down again   a time to shrivel leaving the next generation to get to the top and over

a kiosk contains the book which contains the names of the fallen a perfect record of those boxfuls of bones brittle under caved-in coffin lids under stony soil and lilac sky   this is the burrowing beetles' world that the spider knows nothing of

some died with all their flesh on, some with both eyelids to close over both eyes our young guide has the air of a lover on a postcard smarmed-down hair forget-me-not eyes   a bird flies through the picture *is that a hawk* you ask nervously *a falcon* he replies *without master or jess*

when we tell of our uncle here since 1916 not once disturbed by visitors it takes his breath away, *no one here of that name* he sighs and closes the book later we find the little soldier under an alias of his rascally boyhood

tomorrow this place will be closed for the season, shed padlocked, gates barred   the marching band will sit on the grass polishing brass instruments with khaki rags   at a signal each man will get to his feet preparing his lips for the last blow

while the industrious spider lays her eggs in the body of a beetle strayed into the light

Untitled ("when earth leaps up ...")

when earth leaps up
and heaven descends
and the two meet like lovers
then the question is
could these flowers be stars

and is dust nothing
more than the handful
I sprinkled on your face
as you went down into the dirt

by now I suppose you've crumbled
and your best jacket eaten
by creatures smaller than sandgrains
by creatures so tiny that sandgrains
are their planets this fistful
of earth their universe

they hold hands like children
circling and singing in a playground
you hear them and your elegant bones
turn in the box and as you clap
the carpals of your wrists
fall away from each other

how simple the words to their song
all about blossoming stars
you can join in if you want to

here above ground
all I have left is the question

On Singleness

Today I've become for the first time a lonely woman,
A lonely woman in a woollen skirt and shawl

Moving heavily from one room to another,
Back and forth from the bedroom to the kitchen,

From the kitchen to the storeroom.
I've become someone deciding what to do next,

While the daylight lasts;
What to do next

While the oil lasts for the lamp,
The logs for the stove.

In the crock a half-loaf, in the cupboard
Cheese wrapped in its vinegared muslin,

Two tins of corned beef on the shelf,
In the back of the store five jars

Of lakefish, two of riverfish, berries and
Berries, then mushrooms:

Twenty jars pickled and eleven jars dried,
A small sack of wheat, when opened
Smells softly of mould,

And salt in a block like cattle salt.

I count everything over and over.
I wipe the tops of the jars

I murmur *that's all, that's all.*
I have become an old woman

With cold hands counting jars.
That's all, that's all.

And later out with the maul
To split wood, the last of the wood

That we sawed in the last of the summer.
The block rings like a stone struck.

Shivers of snow fall from the branches.
Above me the usual raven sits in the naked tree,

Croaking his dry claim to my answer.
My dark companion I tell him,

After the logs are split, after the kindling
Is chopped into white slivers,

I shall come with my chipped enamel dishpan
And gather clean snow,

Being careful to keep away from
The bird tracks, the mouse seed,
The rabbit scat.

Nettles

When I am old
I will totter along broken pavements
the strings of my boots undone
smelling a bit strong like any
fat old woman who has forgotten
which day is Tuesday
(my bath night if you like)

stiff my clothes from old dirt
not sweat at my age mumbling
the cracked enamel mug

eleven cats playing
in my weedy yard drinking
my little ration of milk
with me   and withy withy
the cats circle around my house
at night singly filing
in and sleeping on the
saggy stained bed and the chair
and the crumby tabletop

One day they will find me dead
O dead dead
A stinking old bundle of
                                        dead

and in my hand
a peeled wand
and in my ear a cricket sitting
telling me stories and predictions

and the time of night

Flatbread

I have a great mind or I had a great mind once
I used to walk about in a coastal city

or my body when upright
makes an L with the prairie

now I live in a fieldstone hut
some of it has tumbled down
and I believe
in the aesthetic of simplicity

this is my pancake
baked on a hot stone
I have ground the grain myself
it is wild grain
from the shallows of a lake

I fold the pancake over and over and then across
I hold it in the curled palm of my hand
I place it in the empty curve of my mouth
it tastes sweet and gritty
I am satisfied

with my blanket and rock pillow
I prepare for the night

lying in the flat darkness
I dream the corruption of mountains
the splitting of slatey ledges
the crumbling of peaks

Old Woman in Winter

Cup in the hand
Hot cup held in the palm
Almost burning the fingers

But still this is better
Than the dry, dry cold of yesterday
And the day before that

The question is which
Of these days was first
Which will be the last?

To a Friend Dying

these last days
how changeable you are
one moment an old woman
shining and crumpled
as a spring leaf

the next a busty girl
lovers out on the street
can hear you calling them
to your bed

for your comfort
I bring a saltglazed pot
with thornbranch growing
blossoms still furled
in the spiked stem's black nipples

and I tell you the sermon
I shall give at your funeral
"this is only the beginning
of change" I shall say
as I bury your pupa
into its mound of dirt

"on the day of wings
something shall certainly emerge
perhaps not flesh
perhaps not what you expect"

On Wildfire

You are a naked man or woman, all that hair,
Those bunchy clothes stripped like leaves.

Dome-head clockface, the townhall belfry
Sounding like acres of blunted twigs

So like your spread hands. And fishes drowned in air,
Floating and falling scales.

Remember how the spent forest creatures
Crouched strangled by smoky briers.

Remember the plague-cart trundling in the street?
How we dashed in with cloths over our faces?

We didn't ask why this one was wet at the crotch,
Why that one lay clutching a bundle of herbs.

Love's a disease, the last thing he wrote
On the flyleaf of his bible.

On sleeping a man should take off his ring.
Lay it carefully under his pillow.

The wail behind the wind, the whale
Whistling in the deep, over clear water
That rests on ribbed white sand.

Here are sticks and muddy water, you can tear
Your flesh on charred stumps, even in the middle

Of the lake. Next year

You expect August and fireweed,
I expect May and small turrets of Morchella

Pitted Towers of Silence.

Wise Queenie, Wise Queen

Pig poems abound, but Queenie is matchless,
her heartfelt desire for Jack Pig,

her nose in a bucket of swill,
her freedom to root among the tiny potatoes.

Sui, Sui, my love, my love —
that's how I call her to me.

Five piglets, four and a runt,
which she wisely eats.

Next time, she sighs under her warm pigbreath,
all will be voted in — like a parliament.

No, more like a committee of equals. God
if you want to call it that.

Hanner Hwch Hanner Hob – The Flitch

huw from the mountain lover of pigs
comes down for the kill
he who loves truly says huw kills

and he so quiet when he says it
the pig looking up at him
from her little gilt eyes
so you're the one too small to be a mother
says he to the pig called nancy
I can see she trusts him to make
something good of her a useful chine
and sausage   coils of black pudding
beside jellied feet and brawn in the larder

nancy nancy says huw jones
I've made a bed for you see
it's all new straw sweet hay strewn about
lie down my love my beauty lie down *fach*
he says it in welsh of course
how many pigs understand english after all?

and he tells her the tale of the first hogs
how pryderi got them from the lord of ireland
how he kept them styed in the south
how math king of dyfed sent the bard gwydion
to steal them away with his storytelling
his magic and trickery

how the men of the south pursued gwydion
and saturday morning there was a great battle
all because of the pigs see
and when math and his warriors
were bloodying and brawling at the fight
goewin the king's footmaiden was violated
well you wouldn't want that to happen to you
says huw to nancy
the gilt's not so sure she wouldn't
well then darling says huw

and he takes out his sharp little pigknife
and sticks her one
she's gone in a minute
with one happy sigh

when he sees me watching from the pony stall
I could do the same for you *fach* says huw
if I'd just had that much blessing
to be born a pig I tell him
I wouldn't mind it at all

Siôn Forest

look you are this
and this one, a man
with a fine but crooked nose
a woman who wryly says
of her breasts that they are
like those lidded enamel jugs
left at farm gates for
milking-girls to fill
out of kindness
each can with its painted name
Granny Gruffudd, Old Tewdr,
Phylip the Mail, who had
it shot off in the war
and was rewarded
with the perpetual job
of postmaster

and aren't you that man
who got new teeth and cried
with the pain of them
all night and every
night for a week, his wife
rubbing his gums with balsam
weed and bringing him dillwater
in the baby's christening cup?

yes you are that and that one,
Mrs Salisbury, Mrs Jones
come to glean little potatoes
in our hill fields
and Huw from up the mountain
who kills the pigs

and you are the one, Siôn Forest
lying beside me in the night
after the hay's cut and I
awaken in the first hour
of the new day listening

in the storm to the rain
pour down on the mown timothy
and fescue

I can smell dark mildew
already rotting the hay
whose seeds fall damp
and useless to the ground
I count them and they are
as many as you are Siôn
sleeping and waking

The Varying Hare

We shall not all sleep, but we shall all be changed
— 1 Corinthians 15:52

a prayer for the child going to bed
a prayer for his departing
holding in his right hand the enamel
candlestick white with a chipped blue rim
grasping in his left the hem
of his worn nightgown
so as not to fall on the stairs

his brother is allowed to sleep in his clothes
rumpled as they are for fear he may get up at night
and catch his death wherever he can find it

this prayer the mother says to the little one
is simply a defence against creatures
who live at the end of the world
whose snares are like satan's

the child dreams of a rabbit
he dreams his father catches it
with a single looped strand of wire

the big brother lies on his cot
thinking of knowledge got in school
tested in the forest
thinking of himself sitting
at an old oak desk carved with the noble names
of those who long ago marched off to war

his father has told him how they were led away
not to be seen again   probably
they are out there still stepping it
over hill and through marsh
their boots never leaving a print
on wet ground or dry

father the boy says *open the book*
where it tells of the snowshoe hare
her brown coat tipped with white
how lovely she is leaping
and foraging all night
her colours made chalky by the moon
her wary eye on the shadow of an owl

mother the boy writes *it is dawn*
and I have gone into the forest
to visit the hare in her thorny and snowy set
where she sleeps concealed by a tangle
of rose and red osier
god knows nothing can keep her
from the various predators
whose prey she is

tomorrow she may change as we all must
to scrap fur in a tattered bundle

Part Three

Jerusalem

that city of glass these words are printed in the book that lies open before you   I'm reading over your shoulder and cannot see your face but I know that your slightly bulging eyes blue as glass are staring at the page I know that from between those eyes the thought darts out and hits the print with its point that never again will you enter jerusalem

send me I want to tell you but you hush me with the warmth of your hand which is resting on my hand am I cooling your fingers or are you warming mine this question occurs at the same time as conjectures about my journey to that place of iron doors and minarets lighted against the sky whose gates are closed until morning

whose walls are huge blocks of traprock says the book where men in black homburgs weep and wail their tears run down their faces, run down the stones leaving long ribbons of rust

soon I shall scale these walls and enter the city and search up and down the streets for those whose names were once known to you will they put on a false front of flesh will they come shaved and powdered to greet me

or when at last I see them face to face will they turn quickly away and hurry down a sidestreet while one explains to the other a new process for adding gold to the glass of an office building *it's true* he admits that the windows shine rather dully in the sun but then the people inside never have to pull down the blinds for in that place there is neither glitter nor glare but always just enough light to read by

A Sanctuary

There are women living in a house on the mountain, a house that sticks to the rocks as tightly as lichen. At dawn they come out on the bluestone ledge. They stand in lines, a choir singing us awake. Their high voices in unison are a sort of shriek, hard for the teeth to bear.

We look up, and they look down upon us poor primitives in our deep valley not yet enlightened. Look, we say to each other, how cold it is up there. The snow scuds around their feet like an ankle veil.

Snow which hardly ever falls in our valley. If we wanted we could grow potatoes all year long. When it's a bit chilly, we chop down trees and light small fires. A few snowflakes fall into the flames and sizzle to nothing. And perhaps our smoke rises to those holy nostrils, and perhaps it brings tears to those holy eyes.

When we have too many girl children, we send a few babies by rope to those women above. We bundle the little ones in quilted bags, for we don't want them bruised as the sisters haul them up the broken face of the rock.

They say that on the mountain no one has teeth, for there is nothing whatever to chew up there. Ground bones of their dead is what they eat, and sometimes powdered reindeer moss. It's rumoured they suck these delicate meals through straws of ice.

None of us has ever climbed the mountain to speak with these women, for how could we hope to comprehend their wisdom? But we do sometimes stare at them through a makeshift telescope, trying to tell one nun's face from another.

And sometimes a lowly farmer will put his ear to the mountainside, straining to catch the voice of his lost child in prayer, as she kneels in her granite cell, whispering through her puckered mouth cool words of separation and of grace.

The Disc

over and over a woman is told that she's not what
she seems to be   at first she fights this *I am* she
says *what I seem to be:* sand, twigs, stones, and
waves of disturbed air through which a bird has
just flown, also light refracted from the lid of a
syrup tin   the disc of light wobbles on the floor
and ceiling

she begins to have second thoughts   perhaps after
all she is not what she seems: a laurel hedge, a
butterfly flagging on the beach, a scale from the
wing of that butterfly, a rhubarb bush, the oiled
wheel of a train

she could indeed be something not yet mentioned
not yet named *for always* she tells herself *before
you have finished naming a thing the meaning has
changed*   no one can speak as fast as a thought
darts across the mind   no one can speak faster
than the sound of words

I'm not what I seem to be she confesses at last
then a warm subservience floods through her
and she becomes the fluent shadow of any names
we may choose to throw at her

The Elect

Here in the saintly dark, all is so cleanly dank, all is ordered and cradled. Nothing is sinful. Even the suck of the worm's mouth upon us is preordained, therefore right.

Suddenly, it's dawn up there. It comes with the silver squeal of birds, a sound like thin trumpets. "Crack the box," it says. "Arise, this is the day."

Obedient as buds, our heads appear in the open grass, and a rain of golden yods falls down upon us. So this is light. We had forgotten it.

We, who lay long in holy depths of earth, have all at once become small and new, can't even remember our names, and the passers-by won't tell us. They stop. They smile. They stare and then move on.

At last a child in blue cotton leans down to us. "Daffs," she says, and, taking each of us by the neck, yanks for the love of God.

Viaticum – The Text

On the first morning, we saw a road stretching before us, and this road was one long word reaching from here to there. How enticingly clear and simple this seemed. At once, we packed bread and cheese and knives and skins of fresh water and set out with a will upon our journey.

At the close of that day, the road and the word came to an end, and we struck camp for the night. On the second day there was another road, another word. And so it went on. However, at the end of the sixth day things were a little different. Because we had stopped on our way to pick the serviceberries that grew by the side of the road, we arrived late at our camping place. It was already dusk, and we were so tired that we threw ourselves down on the grassy verge without as much as taking off our boots or washing our faces. Indeed, we were so tired that we even forgot our evening prayer to our creator, the Demiurge Y, he who had undoubtedly arranged this journey for us and watched over us as we travelled.

When we awoke, the midmorning sun was hot upon our upturned faces. Above us, in the blue dome of the sky there was not a single cloud, simply a sentence made up of all the words from the past week. The message was simple and direct. As soon as we read it, we fell into momentary despair, for, up to then, we had thought ourselves innocent, or almost so. Truly, we were not deserving of such a judgement.

There was no road and no direction. Would there ever be again? Here we were in the wilderness with no one to guide us. Though our hearts beseeched the Demiurge, he did not heed us. Well, there was nothing for it but to make the best of things, and so we lazed through the day in the long fragrant grass. Even the insects joined us in our rest, and nipped at our skin so gently that we hardly noticed their bites.

Of course Y did not allow us more than one day of rest. The next morning we were off again pursuing the word and the truth with a little less enthusiasm than before, yet still curious to know where the road would eventually lead us.

Now the pattern was set, and we continued for what seemed like centuries in the same way. On every seventh day the week's words were added to those already crowding the sky, and every sentence was more difficult and threatening than the last one. It was not surprising that the Demiurge had decreed a sabbath of rest. We could imagine that it could take him a whole day to compose a suitably abusive judgement for the next week's journey.

As for us mortals, we were glad to stop on the road to fill our flasks with fresh spring water and to enjoy the scenery and the warm sunny weather. When cool evening fell, we began our sabbath dance, watching the shadows of our gestures move gracefully under the moon.

Y was obviously not at all pleased with our lightheartedness, for his words became every week more forbidding and his path more rigorous. In some places it was overgrown with thorny weeds, and in others it was ankle-deep in stinking brackish water. Our creator had made up his mind that we were to travel among the sharp stones, grasping at stinging nettles, and even at poison ivy if we were so foolish as not to recognize its trinity.

One Wednesday morning, as we were wandering along a flinty road that passed through a rockstrewn valley, the enamel sky, which must have become overburdened with the many curses and judgements written upon it, cracked and split into a thousand, thousand pieces. One moment the sky was full of words, the next flakes of blue were falling upon the earth like scurf from the unwashed heads of angels.

And these flakes floated down upon the grass and the stones and the hills and the rivers and the bitter oceans. They alighted too on all the birds and the beasts, even upon our friends the insects. And from this falling all creation received its voice. Never was there such a roaring and a twittering and a buzzing and a squealing. As for us poor wanderers, we too received this blessing. Our ears and our mouths were opened, and we shouted and sang and argued until our throats were sore.

Now there could be no more sky words, and no more need for us to travel the earth. This was the place of our deliverance. We made up our minds to settle in this spot and to build a city with the stones that lay around us. Here we live still, passing the days in discussions and quarrels and the evenings in the singing of bawdy ballads and the telling of tall tales.

No longer are we confined to gesture and the written word. Indeed we have almost forgotten how to read and write so happy are we with the speeches and lies which come effortlessly to our tongues.

As for our master the Demiurge, he has been defeated by his own cruelty and arrogance, for he among all beings did not receive a voice. The sky of words fell downward only, and Y was far too proud to descend from his heaven and accept the gift of speech. In his high place he is silent still, though every now and then he throws down his orders and curses in a written scroll or codex. Of course, we never read these for we are far too busy chatting and boasting and reciting for that.

However, we are not entirely lacking in piety. In the very centre of our city we have built a modest temple to contain these holy objects. Sometimes one of our children, with the natural curiosity of the young, demands to learn to read and to discover the secrets locked up in those pages. Then we gently explain that our revered creator, Yaldabaoth the Demiurge, has promised to punish with terrible severity the impious fool who dares disturb the dusty silence that lies forever upon his words.

Angels

have you noticed
how they roost in trees?
not like birds
their wings fold the other way

my mother, whose eyes are clouding
gets up early to shoo them
out of her pippin tree
afraid they will let go their droppings
over the lovely olive
of the runnelled bark

she keeps a broom by the door
brushes them from the branches
not too gently
go and lay eggs she admonishes

they clamber down
jump clumsily to the wet ground
while she makes clucking noises
to encourage them to the nest

does not notice how they
bow down low before her anger
each lifting a cold and rosy hand
from beneath the white feathers
raising it in greeting
blessing her and the air
as they back away into the mist

Woman Reading in Bath

I am swimming alone on the dark sea
When before me looms up the great stout chin of god
Floating on the black chops of the high tide
And his hands are clutching the slippery wet sides
The edges and the hems of his bungled universe

What's this curling murderously around my neck?
What's this strangling over the blue knots of my neck?
Wiry fingers of hair thick knuckle-bladders
It is a long curled lock from the godhead
Red as sargassum

When the eye is shut then shall the great globe dim
Like a popped bulb scattering flakes
Of slowly falling volcano glass round
The vast bulges of softly swimming belly
And does the great thumping creator's heart
Somehow sit inside and direct the traffic
Of sharks and seals and obedient shoals?
Lucky and cunning from the dark I watch
The huge mouthful of deified teeth from which
Squeaks out a puny cry meant to be a roar
Great heave of the chest but yet a breath
So small it hardly blows my hair about
As I tread water in the shallows
Under the square shadow of his shoulders
He heaves up on stick legs like a fat bird
Crack crack the shanks have snapped
And down he flops on the shingles gasping and stranded

I — the Director — pick up the phone
Connecting me to the sky and the undersea silt
I say *"Birds come down from the clouds"*
I say *"Great crabs come up from the deep*
Chew on this mass — feed all your children
On it for a year"

Oh what a dry and brittle skeleton he makes
But on the last day a small bone hand shall creep
Out of the gray shore sand
And grasping a pebble throw it over my head
Into deep water

Our First Gods Were Fishes

Our first gods were fishes,
for how could we not worship
the elegance of their ribs
the economy of their entrails?

Each spring we watched the passion
of their spawning, saw how their fingerlings
swarmed in the light of the green shallows.

Our lines were twisted hair,
our hooks barbed thorns.

Crouched in the fire's circle
we passed flakes of delicate flesh
from hands to crossed hands, then at a signal
all at once we swallowed our holy ones,
and our bodies became theirs. Our dance
the sudden twist and dash of emerald minnows.

Lately these gods, these fishes
turn up in the interior of split rocks.
Fleshless their bones' white combs.
Valiantly they swim against a current of stone,
opening their mouths to swallow the drought of rock
as though it were the sea.

Now, far from any body
of water sweet or bitter,
we live between the cliffs of the city,
brick walls so high
there's no way of knowing
whether there is anything beyond this
netted trap, this compound
sentence.

Nothing for it but to look upward
to our hope far past the pigeons
burbling on their ledges,
higher even than the falcon's gyre.

And there they are, flying fishes
playfully leaping the blue waves
of upper air, then suddenly regrouping,

Their sober schools
crossing with certainty
the white straits of the clouds.

Procession – The Poem as a Dark Familiar

the presence of the dog her connection to the church
of the ashes the diocese of the holy breath   her
interpretation of stained bones as she gnaws and
tests with her spittle the calx remains of a pitted ulna

she commands a parade to form in the road across
from the hospice   here we jostle for places dragging
garlands that are ripped trees heavy with wilted
leaves

and now the black animal who leads us starts away

she goes before us never turning her head, not that
we expect it, not that we wish it   for it's by faith we
see her muzzle grizzled as it is her eyes red as
poppies

tarum the drum shriek of tin pipes, her way our way
is up the gallow's hill along wet lanes home through
the copse whose dimness slurs her form   thus the
old bitch eludes us enters the sanctuary whose vault
is like the fierce brows of a narrow skull

behind her dusty ears beneath her rough coat
suddenly she is tired of everything, sighs blinks and
sleeps twitching with dreams

sweaty and burdened in our varnished pews we turn
away westward there a priest a stranger is washing
his hands in the font

Theirs Is the Song

i

Seabirds stopped in their flight
are perched on clouds
as on hedges of mist.

Worms lift blunt muzzles
from their beds of sludge;
since the birds are silent
theirs is the song,
rasping as it comes from their mouths'
ten thousand straight pink slits.

A woman walking on the seafront
ties a flimsy scarf round her head
the silk so thin
her wind-burned ears poke through.

She looks up and sees men jump
from their dark moving palace in the sky,
descending like delicate mushrooms
with double stipes.

The sun burns the lips of the waves
until they crisp and fold over,
pancakes ready for jam and cream,
for foam and red tides.

Dead fish have stained the sea
with their amber tears.
Their skeletons are harps of sharp white bones
silent in the mud.

Bubbles prickle the water.
The woman bends. She reads
history from ancient texts scribbled
on the shells swept in by the tide,

stories of dolphin and urchin
coral and shark
smudged by her thumbs.

ii

The reason for the sky is the Earth,
for the Earth the sky.

Somewhere beyond the ether
angels are battling out
that ancient war between colours,
black and white,
silver and gold
their wings.

Their eyes green and grey.
Their open mouths showing red tunnels of song.

Here on Earth we have other things to fight about:
how many shillings in a bag,
how many chimneys make a stack.

Will there ever be a day when we understand
numbers, where they start
and how they flourish and fade?

As for the angels, they have singed their feathers
in the heat of this question:
when exactly does yellow become orange,
where do these two divide?

While in Heaven God struggles with equations,
trying to balance the universe.

iii

How dear to her is the journey of the mind,
flying from dwelling to dwelling,

Her feet scraping the tops of the
forest trees as she floats on by,

Exchanging one language for another,
never quite sure of her bearings,
counting the chimneys on unfamiliar roofs.

One day she hopes to understand progression
how it has no end and no beginning,
how nothing precedes or succeeds,
how time is a disc that wobbles
as it spins.

The melody is an old one
played again and again.
All night she's aware that it scuttles
over the pillows like a louse on holiday.

Waking she hears it emerge from her nose,
a hum like paperwasps.

"But that's just the tune," she says,
"tomorrow on my way I'll write the words."

Malus

I look out the window at a seedling crab which has volunteered in the middle of my windflower patch. How to explain my sudden love for this small but uppity thing?

I'm resolved to watch day by day to make certain that it has everything it needs, rain and grief, sunlight and resignation. I couldn't love it more if I had planted it myself.

When you live in a house like mine where every door opens upon an angel standing on his haloed head and his nightie stiff around his legs, a tower of starched muslin, where every pot on the shelf is home to a tiny priest as small as a spider, his stole about his shoulders ready to hear confession, then you'll know that happiness is the contemplation of outdoor growing things their natural order keyed and adamant.

My darling seedling will you flourish? When you're a sapling will you remember who watered you on dry days? And will I still love you when you're four times my height, your boughs full of blossoms and birdsnests? The blossoms fall and the eggs hatch, such a cheeping and squawking to be fed. Thank God when all are fledged and flying. I was almost ready to pay a woodsman to lop everything to the nub.

Leaves obscure the sky as I pray for bitter apples luminous with knowledge, and, when these are fallen, for enough wasps to feed in the splits and brown bruises, enough buzz to drown out the whirr of the holy man's wheel as he chants cross-legged on the grass under the yellowing leaves, while beside him, its dignity not wavering, sits a black dog lustrous and silent as a monk.

$i^2 = -1$

A chocolate egg is made by binding two equal halves together.

When it is whole, balance it on the pointed end and spin. Eventually it will waver and fall on its side (but which side?) and roll. Never again will you be able to tell which half was right, and which was left.

Or indeed whether the egg is divided N/S or E/W.

But it's true, isn't it, that before something has become a whole we may not refer to it as divided? The trick of a word, the sag of the language, may mean it has always been whole, even before the two halves were joined. Apartness. Agglutination.

Invent me a set of pure symbols. Write me a letter in unmistakeable signs. But are these signs unmistakeable from each other, or are they simply unmistakeably signs?

Now give me an imaginary number; speak me an imagined word.

Resurrection. The tomb opened. An egg broken cleanly, perfectly apart.

Want of Ь Want of Đ

stitch in the side
thorn in the mouth
between tongue and teeth
carmen the glowing carmine of the rose

what happens
going home after the dance?
it's thrown aside
droops its red head
on the gravel of the road
that leads away from the factory

the flower signifies a man at arms
his ceremonial strut
or could be a guerilla lying
at ambush in the long ditch grass

these fall, both cast in the sand
of someone else's glory
while each word held above
the shifting air thins
to less than a syllable

an unvoiced thorn
anther anthem
the easter church
swirls with spring pollen
two young sisters lift their arms
their hands deck the windowsills
with primrose and sallow
catkin exhaling that heady
stink of sap   a veil
for each newly confirmed head
here follows in quires the anthem
rising like smoke
from their virginal fires

mother has clothed them in neat frocks
with wide quaker collars
before summer brings the rose
whose red dye stains the lips
its thorns like cigarettes

what have we left to us
at our age? one sister writes
you wanted to judge
I wanted to pronounce
sentences   neither of us
kept to our maiden calling

(ah the red-stained tongue
between nicotine teeth)

edh edh something always missing
from the mouth   laziness
at the foundry
loss at the font
a blank in the vocabulary
of desire *loth love that tethers thee*
it's a gap grin

and so we lisp on to the grave
sons and daughters follow
the book on the lectern closes
the purple cloth pulled over
the ancient face now fades
the primrose, withers the rose
what was it that we suffered
that we shared?
lack of a letter for an apidental sound?

this sharp and sudden pain in the side
the compositor's error

Skeps in the Orchard

We signed the contract

your part was to lie in the orchard
every afternoon and sleep
mine was to sit and watch you
until you wakened

When autumn came
it was rather chilly for both of us
I folded my shoulders into a blanket
as you slept
your breath rose whitely
into the cool air

The shape of your breath is a cone
it is the shape of inside silence
called null
and from the cone's tip
a word is squeezed out
the word is
worm
worm
worm

the word is latent
the word is fishhook

the word has no sound
it has only a shape
O O O

tip of a needle
is a steel cone
it could get broken
into your finger sewing

it could travel up your arm
and about and around you
until it felt your heart's pull
and pierced itself in

your head is a fat cone
wound with heavy brown hair

or

with soft white hair

or

all the hair could fall out
and show your round head
dull newborn mouse pink
and then a word could be written on your head
with the gray cone tip of a lead pencil

the word is grist
                thistle
                brush
                cerise

words are hive bees
each has the shape of its hum
a winged O

they are flying home in a formation
with the shape of a curved blade
returning to the straw hive
with its knotted tip

A House With a Tower

the Celt within
who likes to stand up and sing
ecstatic and undulating songs
is the one who opens my mouth
and lets the lies out
they buzz like a hum of flies
their flight fills the air
with the beat of gauzy strips, and
Angle, that indwelling cousin,
cannot understand
how all the world is listening
says: *verse is a shelter*
        of blocks that must be built
        carefully for, in the end,
        it may become a palace
        with electric stars

                and together we
                walk solitary
                by a muddy puddle-edge
                (call it a slough)
                looking down into water
                that returns no reflection
                a blank die
                shut eye
                hidden by the dusk
                that creeps up from behind
                my shoulders
                smoking out of the back trees

not hoping for daylight
not for a long time yet

but at morning
here we come
here I come
cry of throat
and twist of tongue

while it has taken Angle years to build his house
hammering beams and attaching tarpaper
tacking it on so carefully

now the liar, I
stand on the tower
shape the sky
with deceiving fingers
while green damsel flies
on their glassy wings rise
infesting the upper air

Some Notes on the Poems

Several of the following notes (the ones indicated by "A.Sz.") were written by the poet.

Our Sullen Art: The title alludes to the poem "In My Craft or Sullen Art" by Dylan Thomas.

Annwfn: "(Welsh) The otherworld, perhaps more of a parallel world than an underworld. Often spelled *Annwn.*" (A.Sz.)

The Fall: "*Hippocastanum,* the horse-chestnut tree." (A.Sz.)

Halinka: A colloquial form of Halina, a girl's name in Polish.

Childermas: The feast of the Holy Innocents, supposedly killed at Herod's command.

Hanner Hwch Hanner Hob: "(Welsh) The title of a story from the *Mabinogion* which tells the tale of how pigs came to Wales." (A.Sz.) "Flitch" is an unsliced side of bacon; "chine" refers to the backbone and adjoining parts of an animal; "gilt" is a young female pig that has not produced a litter.

The Elect: A golden yod is a rare astrological aspect, supposed to be excellent for artistic creativity.

Viaticum — The Text: "Viaticum" means the necessary supplies for a journey (it can also mean holy communion given to someone dying). In some Gnostic traditions, Yaldabaoth is the name of a vengeful creator deity who is jealous of the human soul.

Malus: "*Pyrus malus,* the crabapple tree." (A.Sz.)

$i^2 = -1$: The title is a mathematical equation that helps define an imaginary number.

Want of Þ Want of Ð: "Thorn" and "edh" were letters in Old English, representing "th" sounds (dental fricatives, to use the jargon of linguistics). They are still used in Icelandic.

Bibliographical note

Anne Szumigalski published a total of 16 books, containing more than 270 poems. All of her collections, except for the posthumous *When Earth Leaps Up,* are now out of print.

The poems in *A Peeled Wand* originally appeared in the following books:

Woman Reading in Bath (Doubleday, 1974): Crabseeds, It Wasn't a Major Operation, Long Distance, In the Wilderness, Nettles, Woman Reading in Bath, Skeps in the Orchard

A Game of Angels (Turnstone, 1980): Childermas, Fishhawks, A Game of Angels, Sitting Under Death's Rich Shade, The Name of Our City, Flatbread, Siôn Forest, Angels, A House With a Tower

Doctrine of Signatures (Fifth House, 1983): Our Sullen Art, Annwfn, Frances Walking like a Crane, Shrapnel, Hanner Hwch Hanner Hob — The Flitch, Jerusalem, The Disc, Want of Þ Want of Ð

Instar (Red Deer College, 1985): Sandblind at the Crossing, The Prisoner, The Varying Hare

Dogstones (Fifth House, 1986): Looking for Uncle Tich in the War Cemetery, Procession — The Poem as a Dark Familiar

Journey/Journée (Red Deer College, 1988): On Being a Stranger, On Singleness, On Wildfire

Rapture of the Deep (Coteau, 1991): The Fall, Halinka, The Elect, A Sanctuary, Viaticum — The Text, $i^2 = -1$

Voice (Coteau, 1995): Third Trimester, Voice, Old Woman in Winter, Theirs Is the Song, Malus

Z: A meditation on oppression, desire and freedom (Coteau, 1995; Signature Editions, 2001): "Poem for female voice"

On Glassy Wings (Coteau, 1997): Your Child Looks Up, In Praise of My Own Breasts, Wise Queenie Wise Queen, Our First Gods Were Fishes

Fear of Knives (Hagios, 2000): Fear of Knives

When Earth Leaps Up (Brick, 2006): A Child and His Mother Camp Out on a Cool Night, Untitled ("when earth leaps up"), To a Friend Dying

Biographical note

Anne Szumigalski (née Davis) was born on January 3, 1922, in London, England. Her large family soon moved to a Hampshire village, where she began to write as a child. During the Second World War she worked as an interpreter, medical auxiliary and welfare officer for the British Red Cross, first in England, then on the continent of Europe. Her unit was the first to enter some of the Nazi concentration camps in 1945.

In 1946 she married a Polish emigré, Jan Szumigalski. They would have two daughters and, later, two sons. After spending several years in a remote area of north Wales, the family moved to Saskatchewan, living in the Big Muddy Valley near the U.S. border before settling permanently in Saskatoon in 1956.

Proud to identify herself as a "prairie poet," Anne Szumigalski played a crucial role in the growth of a literary culture in Saskatchewan from the 1960s onward. She was a founding editor of *Grain,* a founding member of the Saskatchewan Writers Guild, a longtime teacher at the Saskatchewan Summer School of the Arts, and the first writer-in-residence at the Saskatoon Public Library. She received a lifetime award for excellence from the Saskatchewan Arts Board, as well as a life membership from the League of Canadian Poets. Apart from such official honours, she was a friend and mentor to dozens of writers in Saskatoon and far beyond.

Anne Szumigalski's first book of poetry, *Woman Reading in Bath,* was published by Doubleday in New York in 1974. Thereafter she chose to have all her work published in Canada. In 1995 she won the Governor General's Award for her collection *Voice.* In her last years both *Arc* and *Prairie Fire* devoted special issues to her work. She died in Saskatoon on April 22, 1999.

ECO-AUDIT

Printing this book using Rolland Enviro 100 Book instead of virgin fibres paper saved the following resources:

Trees	Solid Waste	Water	Air Emissions
2	64 kg	5,064 L	166 kg